**DO NOT REMOVE
CARDS FROM POCKET**

# FACT FINDERS

### Educational adviser: Arthur Razzell

# Photography and Film

### Jonathan Rutland

Illustrated by Ben Manchipp
and Terry Collins F.S.I.A.
Designed by Faulkner/Marks Partnership

Macmillan Education Limited

©1976 Macmillan Education Limited

Published in the United
States by Silver Burdett
Company, Morristown, N.J.
1978 Printing

ISBN 0-382-06241-8

# Photography and Film

# The Eye and the Camera

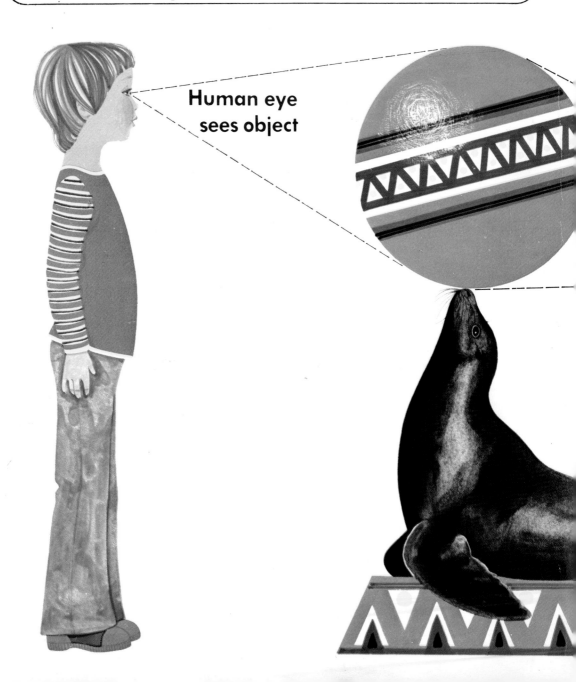

**Human eye
sees object**

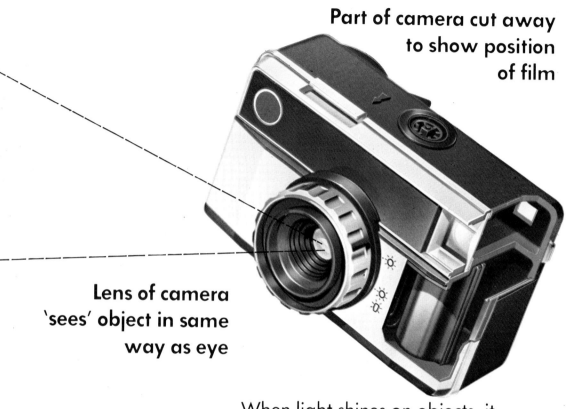

**Part of camera cut away to show position of film**

**Lens of camera 'sees' object in same way as eye**

When light shines on objects, it bounces off them. Light from the objects is reflected into our eyes. This is why we see them.

A camera works in the same kind of way. The lens is the 'eye' of a camera. Light passes through the lens, and is recorded on the film.

# A Moment in Time

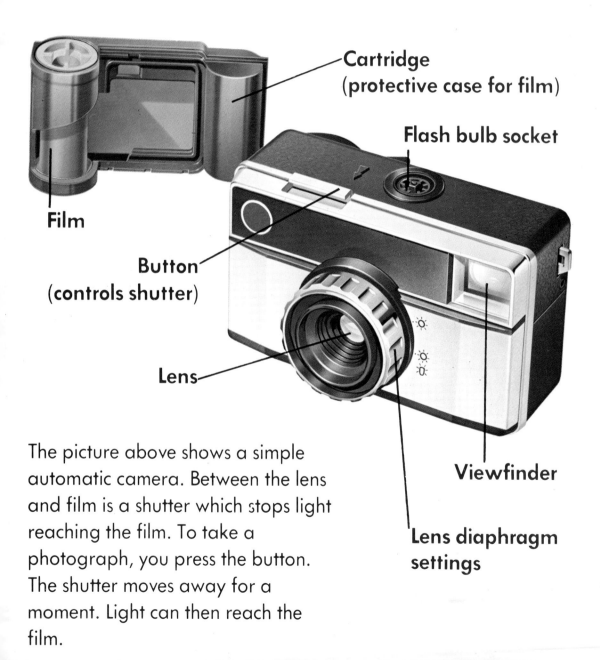

**Cartridge**
**(protective case for film)**

**Flash bulb socket**

**Film**

**Button**
**(controls shutter)**

**Lens**

**Viewfinder**

**Lens diaphragm**
**settings**

The picture above shows a simple automatic camera. Between the lens and film is a shutter which stops light reaching the film. To take a photograph, you press the button. The shutter moves away for a moment. Light can then reach the film.

When we watch something, we can see every movement. A camera only takes a picture of one moment. The photograph (above) shows the children 'frozen' in one moment.

In early photography (right) the shutter was often a piece of card.

# Light and Dark

Eyes let in light through the pupil.
When it is dark, the cat's pupils (below) get larger to let in more light.

In bright sunshine, the pupils become narrow slits.

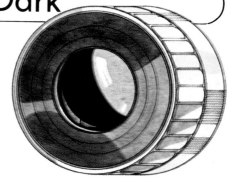

**Lens in dark**

A camera has a diaphragm (dye-a-fram). This does the same job as the pupil. The less light there is, the wider the diaphragm must be opened. The shutter can be left open longer to let in more light.

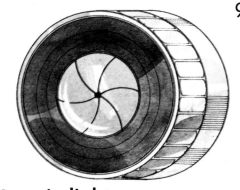

**Lens in light**

# How Film Works

If you lie in the sun for long enough, your skin may turn brown. Photographic film is also affected by light. You can see the effect when the film is developed.

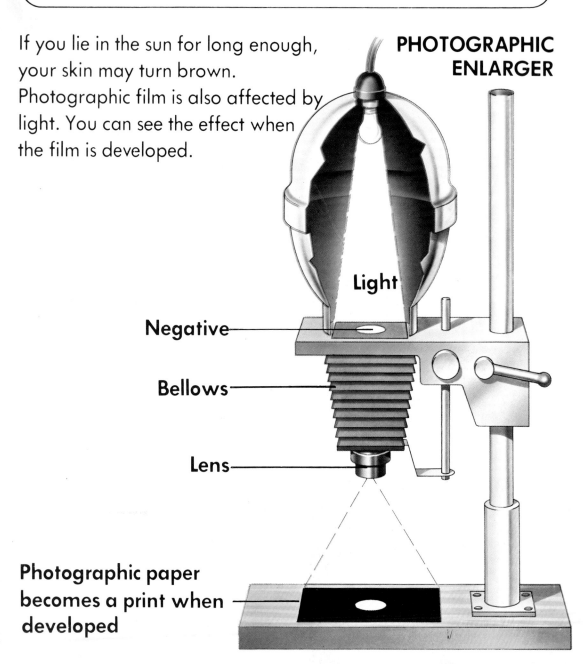

**PHOTOGRAPHIC ENLARGER**

Light

Negative

Bellows

Lens

Photographic paper becomes a print when developed

## 1. Developer contains chemicals to make picture

## 2. Fixer stops picture fading

## 3. Wash (water) cleans print

You make a print from a film negative. Enlargements are made by using an enlarger.

To develop the photograph, you soak it in liquid developer which contains chemicals. Then you soak it in fixer to stop it fading. Finally, you wash the print in water.

# Photography in Action

Some photographers take most of their pictures indoors in a studio lit by bright lights.

On the left is a fashion photographer at work.

A wildlife photographer may take pictures from a hide (below).

The picture on the left was taken from an aircraft at a height of 50,000 feet.

Some cameras take pictures of things that happen too fast for the eye to see. Below, the bullet has just passed through the card.

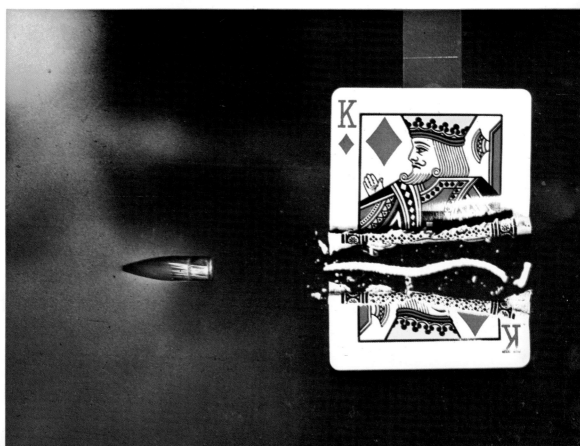

Newspaper photographers must be ready for anything. They often carry several cameras, each with a different lens. The drawing on the right shows how an area can be photographed in three different ways. The photographer can use a telephoto, standard or wide-angle lens.

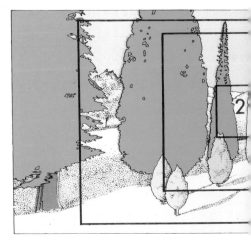

1

**The photograph below was taken by a standard lens (left).**

2

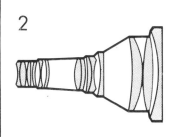

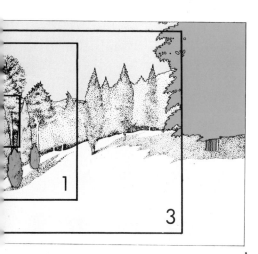

A telephoto lens works like a telescope. It makes objects look nearer and larger. A wide-angle lens takes a very wide scene. It makes things look farther apart than they are.

There are many types of lenses. Some can make straight lines look curved.

**The middle photograph was taken by a telephoto lens.**

3

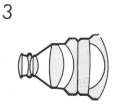

**This photograph was taken by a wide-angle lens (left).**

# Moving Pictures

On the left is a strip of 'frames' from a movie film. Each frame is slightly different. When the film is shown on a screen, the frames follow each other quickly, like a 'flick' book (below). Your eyes see a moving picture.

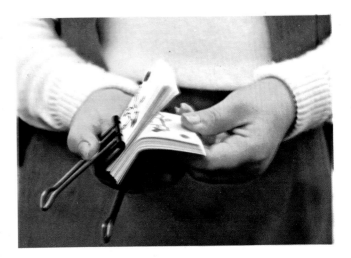

A projector (opposite) has a motor which winds on the film. It also opens the shutter for each frame. It normally projects 22 frames each second.

# Television

A television camera (below) has a lens like other cameras, but no film.

A television camera has a special plate. This plate turns light into electric signals.

The transmitter (above) relays these signals to the television.

The aerial sends them down a wire to the television set. The tube in the set turns the electric signals back into a picture (right).

# Photography at Work

Aerial photographs such as this, are photographs taken from an aircraft. The aircraft flies over the land, and the photographer takes many pictures. Sometimes these pictures are put together and used to make maps.

Special cameras are used for photography under water. They are inside waterproof cases. The controls of the camera are connected to controls on the outside of the case. Powerful lights are needed as it is very dark under water.

# Glossary

**Developing**   Making a picture appear on photographic film or paper by using liquid developer.

**Enlarger**   An instrument for making large photographs from small negatives.

**Film**   Special material which is affected by light. The brighter the light, the more the film is affected.

**Fixer**   A chemical used to stop photographic film or paper being affected by light after it has been developed.

**Flash Bulb**   A bulb that makes a very bright flash, for taking photographs in dim light.

**Frame**   A single photograph on a movie film.

**Lens**   A curved piece of glass. Light passes through the lens on to the film.

**Negative**   A photograph where the light parts of the picture are dark and the dark parts are light.

**Photographic Paper**   Special paper which is affected by light.

**Print**   A photograph printed on paper.

**Shutter**   A piece of metal behind the lens of a camera. It stops light reaching the film.

**Viewfinder**   The eyepiece of a camera. If you look through a viewfinder, you can see the part of the scene that will appear on the film.

# Index

1 2 3 4 5 6 7 8 9 10— R —85 84 83 82 81 80 79